Original title:
Through the Living Room Window

Copyright © 2025 Creative Arts Management OÜ
All rights reserved.

Author: Seraphina Caldwell
ISBN HARDBACK: 978-1-80587-010-4
ISBN PAPERBACK: 978-1-80587-480-5

Dreams Carried by the Wind

A squirrel wears a tiny hat,
Dancing on the fence post fat.
He juggles acorns in the air,
While birds all stop to stop and stare.

The curtains flap as breezes shift,
A joyful scene, a comic gift.
Neighbors gather with their drinks,
At the odd parade, no one thinks.

Bathed in Twilight Reflections

The cat pretends to be a lion,
As shadows stretch and curtains flyin'.
A moth, like a chatty guest,
Flits around—won't give it rest.

Lights flicker on with a soft glow,
While a dog barks at the shadow show.
Cupcakes cool on the window sill,
A laugh escapes—what a sweet thrill!

A Patch of Sky

A patch of blue so brilliantly clear,
Where clouds play tag without any fear.
In the background, a loud cat meows,
While plants poke heads from garden bows.

A bird dives low, it's quite the sight,
Chasing the sun as day turns to night.
Laughter spills from a yard nearby,
As a child leaps, aiming to fly.

Flickers of Time Passing

The clock ticks loudly—oh so slow,
While paperboats in puddles flow.
A child runs fast, with sticky hands,
Creating silly, splashing plans.

Old chairs creak with each weary sigh,
As stories unfold, the laughter flies.
Mom's cake collapses, it wobbles then falls,
As the sound of giggles fills up the halls.

Stillness in Motion

A cat leaps high, then lands with grace,
While socks take flight in an unseen race.
The world outside is a bustling show,
But here, it's a circus that steals the glow.

The mailman dances with every stride,
A dog barks back, full of canine pride.
Birds flit like thoughts escaping my head,
While I sip my coffee, still half in bed.

The Threshold's Embrace

At the door, a face peeks, curious and small,
It's the neighbor's kid, asking, 'Can I play ball?'
With toys scattered wide like confetti from fun,
I nod and we tumble, two for the price of one.

Dad's caught in socks, a silly mishap,
Trying to juggle his morning nap.
We laugh at the chaos, the racket, the cheer,
Wishing these moments could last through the year.

Moonlight Through the Veil

The moon winks down, a lighthearted tease,
As I trip over sneakers, down on my knees.
Shadows do tango, an odd kind of fun,
While star-gazing dogs chase, panting, then run.

A light flickers on, illuminating the night,
As I share conspiracies with a pile of fright,
The fridge hums a tune, a lullaby sweet,
Carrots and cake in a midnight retreat.

Fractured Perspectives of Home

With each passing car, stories collide,
A family of squirrels is joyfully fried.
Dad's hair is wild, like a tornado blew,
While Mom swats the fly with a rogue shoe.

The couch throws a party with cushions galore,
And the laughter spills out as I reach for the floor.
Windows click softly, each glance a fresh scene,
In the zany parade where life's ever keen.

Nature's Canvas

Leaves dance lightly in the breeze,
Colorful hues that tease and please.
Squirrels hold silly acorns tight,
While birds pick outfits for their flight.

A butterfly flits, just out of reach,
Chasing the cat who's lost in speech.
Dandelions wave hello to bees,
As daisies gossip with the trees.

Echoes of Laughter Outside

Children caper with joyful screams,
Chasing each other and daydreams.
A dog decides to join the fun,
Pawing through puddles, oh what a run!

Neighbors chuckle, sharing a bite,
While one attempts to take flight.
Balloons escape into the sky,
As folks below just laugh and cry.

The Stillness Between Us

Two chairs sit side by side,
Filled with memories that can't hide.
Laughter echoes from days gone by,
While old jokes still make us sigh.

A gentle breeze stirs silent air,
As if the world is unaware.
Comfy cushions whisper sweet tales,
Of naps and jokes and fairy fails.

Raindrops etching Stories

Pitter-patter on the glass,
A symphony of sounds as they pass.
Each drop a tale of journeys taken,
Of umbrellas turned into bacon!

Puddles form a dance floor grand,
Where rubber boots take their stand.
Splashes echo with pure delight,
As rain joins in the joyful fight.

A Slice of the Everyday

A bird lands awkwardly, much to my delight,
Its flapping looks more like a clumsy flight.
It steals my crumbs, oh what a sight!
While I sip my tea, everything feels just right.

The neighbor's cat glances with such attitude,
As if judging my taste in afternoon food.
A grin spreads wide as it rolls in the sun,
Gossip from my chair, life's little fun.

The Watching Eye

A squirrel darts fast, a master of stealth,
Searching for treasures, so full of mischief, it's wealth.
It stops to stare, our gazes collide,
I crack a smile; it looks back with pride.

The mailman trips over a flower bed,
A ballet of flailing, what's in his head?
With packages flying, dog barks like a fool,
Oh, what a scene—life's unpredictable school!

Threads of the Outside World

Children laugh, their antics too bold,
Jumping in puddles, their joy uncontrolled.
Each splash is a masterpiece, painted bright,
While I sit and chuckle, a cozy delight.

A jogger trips over a curious toy,
It's a bright red truck—a child's pure joy.
He shakes his head, laughs, then runs on his way,
Turning mundane moments into playful ballet.

An Invitation to Wonder

The world outside dances in vibrant hues,
As shadows stretch long in the evening's blues.
An old dog snores, while ants march in line,
Together they script a tale that's divine.

Each glance outside pulls me into their play,
Who knew the mundane could brighten my day?
With laughter as my guide, I open my eyes,
Adventures await beneath ordinary skies.

Where Time Meets Tranquility

In the quiet of a sunny nook,
A cat yawned wide, a playful look.
The clock ticks slow, while tea cups sway,
As hours dance and drift away.

Outside, the world does somersaults,
While squirrels wage their daring vaults.
A breeze plays tricks, the curtains sway,
In this stillness, time's at play.

Daydreams on the Edge of Reality

A neighbor's dog wears mismatched socks,
He guards the yard, a noble fox.
The sun dips low, a golden glow,
As laughter drifts from all below.

Kids chase bubbles, shouting loud,
A musical mishap—call the crowd!
The pizza guy arrives on cue,
With toppings wild, a strange review.

Nature's Canvas in Focus

Birds paint the sky in vibrant hues,
While clouds rearrange like wacky crews.
A garden gnome looks rather sly,
As bees buzz by, oh my, oh my!

The roses gossip, petals aflutter,
A snail takes its time, with no need to clutter.
Sunlight winks through the leafy veil,
As nature tells its funny tale.

The Story Beyond the Glass

A pigeon struts, like it owns the street,
With swagger so grand, it can't be beat.
A man walks by, with mismatched shoes,
In this panorama, laughter ensues.

The wind whispers secrets, gently it hums,
While mashed potato clouds softly come.
Each moment outside, a curious blend,
Of silliness and joy, around every bend.

Serene Moments in the Chaos

A cat sprawls, a dog barks loud,
Kids racing by, a bus, a crowd.
Coffee spills, and laughter sings,
In this chaos, joy still clings.

A squirrel darts, leaves dance up high,
Birds gossip, their wings spread wide.
Plants in pots all lean with glee,
As the world spins, oh let it be!

Echoing Footsteps on the Sidewalk

Evening strolls, the ducks parade,
Someone slips, but plans won't fade.
Neighbors wave, they shout a tease,
One trips over a bag of peas.

Laughter blends with honking cars,
As dishes clatter behind closed bars.
Pigeons strut, puffed up with pride,
In this chaos, life won't hide!

Misty Memories at Dusk

Curtains sway, a breeze comes in,
Tales of old, where to begin?
Grandma's hat, a tale unraveled,
In the dusk, memories traveled.

Moths collide with the glowing light,
A dance of shadows, quite a sight.
A sneaky dog takes a quick nap,
While the world grows soft with a wrap.

Flashes of Life Intertwined

Neighbors share their quirky cheer,
While a toddler giggles near.
A bird arrives to steal a fry,
As popcorn flies and someone sighs.

Old folks chat of times long past,
While family bonds are built to last.
Each laugh echoes, spins 'round and round,
In these moments, joy is found!

Another Afternoon Unraveled

The cat jumps high, a mighty leap,
Chasing dust motes, no time for sleep.
A knock at the door, who could it be?
A friend with snacks, oh joy, oh glee!

Socks on the floor, they dance in the air,
We laugh as we trip—there's chaos to share.
A game of charades in the flickering light,
Our goofy antics, a hilarious sight.

The Inviting Glow of Home

The clock strikes six, popcorn starts to pop,
Couch potato kingdom, we never want to stop.
With slippers on and blanket draped tight,
We plot our next heist for the midnight bite.

Outside, the stars twinkle, their bright little eyes,
Inside, we chuckle, oh how time flies!
The fridge is our compass, the guide of our fate,
We battle for nachos, it's never too late!

Conversations with the Breeze

The window is open, a breeze whispers through,
The curtains are dancing, it's quite the view.
We chat with the clouds, gossip all around,
Nature's our audience, symphonic sound.

A squirrel on the branch, a cheeky little tease,
We wave to the neighbor while sipping our teas.
"Did you see that raccoon? He stole my last fry!"
Laughter erupts, as the day flutters by.

When Time Stands Still

The clock sits frozen, what time can it be?
We've lost all track, just your friend and me.
With games and giggles, we forget the hour,
We're wrapped in the joy, the world's lost its power.

Silly faces, we pull, oh what a delight,
As shadows stretch longer, teasing the night.
The golden light fades, but we're far from done,
In our little haven, we've already won.

Reflections in the Silhouette

A cat on the sill, plotting his scheme,
Chasing the shadows, living his dream.
But the sun sneezes bright, and what a surprise,
He leaps in the air, then hides from his prize.

The neighbor's dog dances, in wild, joyous glee,
While I sip my coffee, oh what a sight to see!
They exchange silly glances, a comical show,
Who knew a little window could spark such a glow?

Chasing Clouds from the Couch

Pillow fort kingdoms, where dreams take their flight,
With clouds made of marshmallows, dazzling and white.
A toss of the popcorn, it rains on the floor,
As giggles escape from behind the couch door.

The world outside beckons with bright, friendly skies,
But who needs the outdoors when we've crafted our lies?
With every new cloud, we paint stories untold,
As plush toys join in, with antics so bold!

The Window's Whispered Tales

The curtains like storytellers, sway and they dance,
As squirrels scamper by, not leaving to chance.
A knock of the breeze sends the papers in flight,
While I chuckle and wonder what's causing this plight.

Glimpses of life on the street fill the air,
A jogger who trips, what's he doing out there?
Each moment a tale, played out with wild flair,
The window just giggles; it loves to share care!

Sights Unraveled at Dusk

At dusk when the world wears a shimmery cloak,
Bugs buzzing secrets, or maybe just smoke.
A raccoon in the garden, waving hello,
While the flowers conspire in whispers, so low.

The sun yawns and stretches, painting the scene,
As shadows grow longer, the frogs join the keen.
With a leap and a croak, they break into song,
Oh, who needs a concert? This chaos feels strong!

Where Light and Life Converge

Sunshine spills on my old cat's chin,
He licks and struts in a regal spin.
Squirrels plotting with acorn hats,
Who knew my yard was a drama for cats?

The neighbor's dog gives a loud woof,
As kids pass by, I can hear their goof.
An ice cream van, its tune a delight,
Chasing dreams on a Saturday night.

The wind dances with laundry on the line,
Making my socks look like they shine.
A bird lands with a quizzical stare,
I swear we share secrets in the air.

Even my goldfish seems to agree,
Life's a show, just wait and see.
With every glance, the world feels new,
Who knew the laughter would come from the view?

The Rhythm of Passing Days

The clock ticks steady, but oh so slow,
Curtains flutter, an animated show.
Neighbors bicker with feisty glee,
I chuckle softly, they're loud as can be.

A rogue leaf slams against the pane,
I laugh, it's like nature's own campaign.
Traffic sings its own off-key tune,
A symphony brought alive by the moon.

Children play ball, dodging in sight,
With joyous shouts that ring day and night.
I sip my tea, watching all unfold,
A silent witness to stories untold.

As shadows stretch, the sun dips down,
Colors splash like a painter's crown.
Each moment blends into a vibrant swirl,
In this comedic dance, I watch and twirl.

Nature's Embrace Beyond My Reach

Raindrops race down the window's glass,
Like tiny athletes in a swift pass.
Flowers lean in, almost to peek,
At the shenanigans of kids down the street.

A snail creeps by with a shell so grand,
While ants march forth, a busy band.
The grass waves secrets that tickle my feet,
Nature's gossip, oh how sweet!

A squirrel slips on the garden swing,
I laugh so hard, what joy does he bring!
Butterflies are the fairies of flight,
Dancing in colors that feel just right.

Even the clouds join the fun above,
Puffing and primping, it's a show of love.
Life spins on, just outside my door,
This quirky world, who could ask for more?

The Art of Watching

Peeking outward, the show begins,
Birds in bow ties, debutants of spins.
A raccoon raiding a picnic feast,
I can't help but laugh at the little beast.

With popcorn ready and cozy chair,
I'm front row to this wild affair.
Hats off to the sun for its golden light,
A spotlight on chaos, what a delight!

An old couple waltzes with lawn chairs,
Throwing glances as sweet as paires.
I jot down ideas for my next doodle,
Inspired by life's loving, soft poodle.

The curtain falls when evening's near,
As fireflies flicker, they bring good cheer.
In silent applause, I tip my hat,
To the whimsical world, that's where I'm at.

Patterns of Time in the Glass

The cat lies sprawled, with dreams of tuna,
Birds outside squawk, causing quite the drama.
Sunlight dances, a golden ballet,
While I sip tea, watching the fray.

Strangers pass, with phones in hand,
One trips over grass, oh isn't life grand?
A toddler's giggle, a dog's sudden bark,
Creating a symphony in the park.

The mailman waves, while juggling his load,
A paper airplane, oh look, it just glowed!
That neighbor in plaid, with socks full of holes,
Is dancing like no one, shaking his poles.

Mom shouts, "Dinner!" from the smell of the stew,
But I'm lost in the chaos, oh what shall I do?
With laughter and quirks unpacked every day,
Life through this portal is silly, hooray!

Reflections of a Wondered Heart

A squirrel in a hat, how bizarre, I think,
As it wobbles and hops, ready to blink.
The sunlight shines bright, like glitter in cheer,
While I scratch my head, wondering what's near.

My neighbor's laundry, a colorful sight,
Flapping in the breeze, oh what pure delight.
Are those polka dots, or some kind of beast?
Guess the washing machine had quite the feast!

The mailboxes chat, whispering secrets,
Sharing their tales of mundane regrets.
"Did you see who backed up? A vintage old car!"
"Uh-oh, it's rolling, better watch it from afar!"

As shadows grow long, the day bows and bends,
I chuckle at the world and all its odd ends.
Each glance out this view gives life a new start,
With giggles and quirks, it tickles my heart.

An Open Book of Life

A cat sprawls, tail flicking light,
While birds tease from their lofty height.
The dog rolls over, chasing a dream,
With squirrels plotting a cheeky scheme.

Oh, what a tale this room can spin,
With echoes of laughter where joy begins.
Bouncing shadows dance on the wall,
As the family chaos embraces us all.

Caught between the dishes and laughs,
Each heart a snippet, a photograph.
The couch a stage, where thoughts collide,
In this wild screenplay where we abide.

As laughter leaks from every nook,
Life's simply an open book.
With every glance, a story unfolds,
In this cozy den, where life never grows old.

Fleeting Glances of Joy

A burst of giggles from the floor,
As toddlers tumble and beg for more.
Mom spills coffee with a dramatic flair,
While Dad pretends he's unaware.

Here come the neighbors with pie in hand,
Surely they've come to seek a stand.
It's an impromptu feast at half-past two,
Where secrets are whispered and laughter ensues.

A dog in socks skids across the tiles,
As we pause to wear our biggest smiles.
Life is brief, yet moments stick,
Like frosting on shirts from a cupcake pick.

Through fleeting glances, joy weaves tight,
In the tapestry woven of pure delight.
Each day bursts forth with colors anew,
In this vibrant scene where fun is the glue.

Seasons' Secrets Beneath the Eaves

The autumn leaves sweep past the glass,
While kids flicker shadows that dart and pass.
A pumpkin's grin from the porch steps,
Hints at the mayhem the season preps.

Winter whispers with a frost-kissed breath,
Noses pressed close, it's magic or death.
Snowmen wobble as they stand quite proud,
Mocking the families gathered in crowd.

Spring sneaks in with flowers ablaze,
A chorus of laughter on sunny days.
The dog finds mud in a comical dance,
As we marvel at bloom, and take a chance.

Summer hums with a joyful tune,
As we sip lemonade beneath the moon.
Secrets flutter like curtains in air,
Giving warmth to us all, like a loving care.

Whirlwinds Beyond the Threshold

A whirlwind comes, and whiskers twitch,
As tripping feet make quite the pitch.
The doorbell rings, and the chaos falls,
With laughter ricocheting off the walls.

Neighbors popping in for a brief hello,
With tales embellished, oh, the flow!
Jokes about dogs chasing their tails,
And the ups and downs of our daily trails.

A game of charades spins wildly 'round,
With arms flailing as giggles abound.
Life is a circus, a colorful show,
Where silliness reigns, and joy tends to grow.

Just outside, life bustles and spins,
While inside, it's mischief that always wins.
In this lively room, where stories blend,
We find humor and love that never ends.

The Energy Outside My Haven

Laughter spills from the yard,
Children racing, laughter loud,
A dog in a cowboy hat,
Chasing after clouds.

Squirrels plotting on a limb,
Stealing snacks with sneaky grace,
A pigeon eyeing my sandwich,
With a very judgmental face.

The gardener croons a sweet tune,
While bees buzz their afternoon jam,
A cat performs a daring leap,
On the fence to claim her fam.

A family barbecue ignites,
With burgers flipping, smoke a-blur,
Someone tripped on their own two feet,
And landed right in the stir.

Fragrance of the Evening Air

The scent of grilled delights,
Drifting through the sleepy street,
A blend of spices and laughter,
With a neighbor's dog at my feet.

Fireflies flicker and tease,
Like tiny stars that land on grass,
A chorus of crickets sings loud,
While I watch the neighbors pass.

The ice cream truck's melody plays,
Each child dashes, a wild stampede,
Coins clutched tightly in small hands,
As dreams of sprinkles take the lead.

The gentle breeze carries joy,
Twirling leaves in playful motion,
A world alive at twilight's hour,
Awash in simple commotion.

A Dance of Silhouettes

In the dusk, they come alive,
Shadows waltz upon the ground,
Two lovers twirl, side by side,
A dance of joy, without a sound.

A dog strikes a pose mid-leap,
Chasing his own wiggly tail,
While a squirrel does a grand jig,
In a nutty ballet of scale.

In the haze, a toddler trots,
Her arms flapping, a clumsy rhyme,
As two birds argue overhead,
Over peanuts lost in time.

Lawn chairs bob like restless seas,
While shadows stretch and curve and glide,
A whimsical ballet unfolds,
In the evening's gentle tide.

Glimpse of a Neighbor's Smile

The curtain parts, just a crack,
A fleeting grin across the way,
Mr. Johnson with a cookie jar,
Caught sneaking sweets at midday.

She's watering plants, with flair,
Wearing bright polka dots so bold,
Her parrot squawks a greeting,
As I wave, my story told.

A child peers out with big eyes,
Searching for the ice cream truck,
His face lights up with sheer delight,
As he twirls, just pure luck.

From my seat, I catch it all,
A tapestry of silly sights,
Neighbors sharing moments sweet,
In the chorus of warm nights.

Cradled by Comfort

In the corner, the cat takes a leap,
Chasing the dust that begins to creep.
Mom's voice floats, a familiar sound,
Where snacks and laughter are always found.

Grandpa snores in his armchair throne,
While the TV buzzes a constant drone.
Kids playing tag, then hiding fast,
In a world where fun forever lasts.

A plant bends low for a sip of sun,
Its leaves too heavy, the battle won.
Outside the chaos, a neighbor's cat,
Strolls by nonchalant, oh look at that!

Bubbles float from the dish nearby,
Popping soft with a sugary sigh.
In this space of warmth and cheer,
Time dances on with nothing to fear.

Silhouettes Against the Glow

As twilight falls, the shadows play,
Dancing figures in a whimsical ballet.
The dog's nose twitches, caught in a dream,
Chasing the moonbeams that spark and gleam.

Children giggle, the floor becomes lava,
Jumping from cushions, oh what a drama!
A sippy cup splashes, a soda can fizz,
Oops, let's mop it—where is the whiz?

Outside the glow, a couple holds hands,
While we craft stories in makeshift bands.
The clock ticks loudly, but we don't care,
In this silhouette dance, we float on air.

Every lamp is a beacon, each shadow a friend,
With every twist, a new tale to send.
Laughter erupts, like wildflower blooms,
In the warmth of this home, joy always looms.

Stories Told in Shadows

Upon the wall, the stories grow tall,
Tales of dragons and big marching balls.
A flick of the hand starts a new plot,
Unfolding mysteries in every spot.

A bear in a top hat, sipping tea,
While a turtle dressed sharp negotiates glee.
Grandma's laughter ignites the air,
As bedtime stories turn into a fair.

The dog, a knight, guards the shoe pile,
Dreaming of battles in heroic style.
And there, the shadows of kids dance wild,
Each one scribbling fancy, a whimsical child.

The laughter fades but echoes will stay,
In this cozy realm where shadows play.
Tomorrow we'll weave more tales to ignite,
Adventures await with the morning light.

The Gentle Caress of the Seasons

Spring's sneak peek through the fabric seams,
 Joyful sunbeams and daydream streams.
A breeze flutters curtains like tickling hands,
While outside the kiddie pool takes its stands.

Summer's mischief with popsicle drips,
 Stealing sweet fruit from the lunchbox tips.
 The dog rolls over, sun-spotted and hot,
 Spoiled by warmth in this cozy spot.

Autumn sneezes, leaves spin and swirl,
 A raucous dance in a golden twirl.
 Pumpkins and cider, stories replete,
 As sweaters emerge, oh isn't it neat?

Winter giggles with frosty delight,
 Hot cocoa hugs, and snowball fights.
Each season whispers what memories yield,
In this room of comfort, our hearts are sealed.

The World Unfolds Beyond

Cats in pajamas strut around,
Dancing like they own the ground.
Squirrels playing hide and seek,
Chasing shadows, oh what a week!

Neighbors argue over the fence,
While dogs plot their own mischief hence.
A bird drops a snack on my head,
I laugh as daylight stumbles ahead.

The mailman trips on a garden gnome,
While kids race past in a sugar-filled foam.
Laughter echoes in the afternoon light,
In this curious world, all feels just right.

From my chair, I sip my tea,
Watching the chaos so wild and free.
Life's a show, the curtains drawn,
And every day feels like a dawn.

Shadows Dancing on the Wall

Shadows twirl like they're in a ballet,
Mice holding a kitchen soiree.
A lamp flickers, plays peek-a-boo,
While the cat ponders what next to pursue.

Dust bunnies tumble like acrobats,
Jumping and rolling, oh where are the cats?
A stray sock joins the floor parade,
Where every day is a new charade.

Dishes sing their favorite song,
As I reach for a chip, it goes wrong!
The fridge hums a melody of its own,
Creating a symphony in my so-called throne.

In this room, life gets its groove,
Every little detail starts to move.
With every glance, a giggle unfurls,
In the dance of shadows, my heart twirls.

Glimpses of Life Beyond the Pane

Bicycles zoom like racing cars,
While kids turn their heads to the stars.
Lawn flamingos stand guard so proud,
As my neighbor sweeps, feeling quite loud.

A toddler throws tantrums with glee,
While a dog steals a sandwich for tea.
Sunlight spills like laughter all around,
Streaming through cracks where joy is found.

The ice cream truck's jingles play on repeat,
Sparking delight in both child and street.
A cat in a hat looks quite confused,
In this comedy show, I've been bemused.

As the day fades like a well-told joke,
I sit back and share a chuckle with folk.
Every glimpse is a giggle waiting to be,
In this world so lively, so wild, and so free.

Views from My Sanctuary

The world is a circus, and I have the best seat,
With popcorn and soda, life feels so sweet.
Neighbors argue, their antics a play,
While I giggle, enjoying my day.

A poodle prances in a polka-dot coat,
While the postman's shoe decides to float.
Barbecues sizzle in the summer haze,
And laughter erupts in the golden rays.

A squirrel fashions a hat from my shoe,
While I ponder just what I should do.
The garden blooms with colors so bright,
Every day feels like a spontaneous light.

As twilight descends with its painterly thread,
I raise my mug for the laughter I've bred.
Views from my fortress of comfort and cheer,
In this amusing world, I hold dear.

Reflections of a Quiet Afternoon

The cat naps wide on the sill,
Dreams of chasing a rogue quill.
Birds debate who gets the crumbs,
While I sip tea and count the hums.

A squirrel darts, then does a flip,
Right into the neighbor's flower trip.
Laughter erupts from my cozy chair,
As I watch chaos with utmost care.

A passing dog dons a silly hat,
Chasing its tail, oh where's it at?
Children giggle, play tag near the fence,
Their vibrant joy is just immense.

The world outside is a grand show,
Full of antics, all aglow.
I chuckle softly, my heart in glee,
What a circus for just me!

Whispers from the Outside

A leaf falls down with a crispity crack,
The mailman fumbles, can't find his stack.
A dog next door gives a loud, proud bark,
As I snicker at the chaos, bright and stark.

Kids on bikes zoom past with glee,
One hits a bump, 'Oh, not again!' he plea.
Laughter echoes with every fall,
And I can't help but chuckle through it all.

A squirrel prances, all filled with sass,
As it tries to steal from the green grass.
A bird mocks from the highest tree,
With a chirp that tickles, oh so free.

The world is a stage, this I know,
With giggles and mishaps all in a row.
Through the pane, life's theater unfolds,
A delightful scene, so full of gold.

A Portal to the Day

Sunlight spills like spilled milk on the floor,
As the world wakes up and starts to explore.
I see a mail truck in a dance of wheels,
Delivering laughter and crazy feels.

Waves of teenagers, music on blast,
Skateboards flying, oh how they go fast!
One almost tumbles, pulls off a stunt,
And the cheers burst forth, oh what a front!

A bird suits up in a tuxedo of grey,
Pecking the ground as if to say,
'My dinner's here, and it's quite a feast!'
I laugh at the sight, my joy increased.

Every glance outside is pure delight,
Filled with spills of humor, morning light.
Life parades by, so whimsical and weird,
From my little spot, it's all that I've cheered.

Sunbeams on Wooden Floors

Warm rays invade this cozy nook,
The world outside, a storybook.
A cat gives chase to a beam of light,
Paws flailing, what a foolish sight!

Dandelions sway with playful mirth,
While children discover a tin can worth.
They're building castles out of thin air,
Each topple brings giggles, oh what a flare!

The neighbor spills paint all over the walk,
With colors that argue, they begin to talk.
A booming voice yells, 'Now that's quite bold!'
Making art as the laughter unfolds.

Sunbeams dance as the moments pass,
Each funny mishap composes the glass.
From my perch, I soak in the cheer,
As the world spins tales that bring me near.

Moments Caught in Stillness

A cat on the sill, watching a bird,
One flick of a tail, the chase is absurd.
A squirrel does dance, all clumsy and spry,
While the dog, with a sigh, just watches nearby.

Neighbors appear in their sweats and their hats,
A jogger does trip, flipping past all the mats.
The postman arrives, with a smirk on his face,
Too bad his delivery has gone out of pace.

The kid on the bike rides far too fast,
Him wobbling and squeaking, it's a real blast.
A toddler throws toys with glee on the floor,
As a forgotten shoe rolls right out the door.

In this small frame, life plays a sweet jest,
Moments of laughter, we treasure the best.
Time pauses, then skips, like a record that's stuck,
Oh the joy in the chaos, oh the laughter, oh luck!

Muffled Music from Afar

A tune wafts in, half cool, half bizarre,
From the neighbors' party, they're strumming guitars.
The dog howls along, it's a concert for two,
While I sip tea as they belt out the blues.

The elderly couple does shuffle and sway,
Trying to dance like it's back in their day.
One foot gets tangled, a flip and a flop,
As the laughter erupts, they won't ever stop.

Kids on the block, with their scooters parade,
Bumping and crashing, it's a comical charade.
I chuckle and cheer, through the echoing night,
A blend of sweet chaos, it's pure delight.

This melody shared, with its giggles and pings,
Turns the ordinary into joyful things.
No need for a ticket, just sit back, unwind,
In this free show of life, unexpected and kind.

Nature's Drama on Display

The trees have a talk, rustling leaves like a play,
A squirrel steals center stage, scurries away.
Birds chirp their lines, in a cacophony bright,
As a butterfly flutters, a true aerial sight.

The sun peeks out shyly, through clouds stacked so high,
While raindrops decide if they're coming by.
A thunderclap roars, then fades with a grin,
And a spider spins dreams on a silken string.

The flowers all gossip, colors clash and collide,
Bees buzz in the mix, in a sweet, sticky ride.
A pair of raccoons engage in a heist,
As the world's nature comedy plays out, unleashed.

In this constant theater, so lively, so strange,
Every glance through this frame feels utterly deranged.
Life's funny, chaotic, a role that we play,
Nature's silly antics steal breath away.

The Veil of Glass

A snowflake drifts down, then lands with a thud,
The branches all bow, greeted by the flood.
I chuckle as puddles reflect the sky's blue,
While the world outside dances, it welcomes the dew.

A fly lands and zooms, then gets lost in a spin,
While the cat makes a lunge, amusement begins.
She pounces on air, with an acrobatic jest,
While I laugh out loud, a spectator at best.

The postman arrives with a card that he flings,
It spirals and twirls like it's learning to sing.
Then a gust of strong wind sends it far, just in time,
And I can't help but chuckle, oh what a rhyme!

Behind this thin barrier, life's oddity shines,
Moments of humor blend with awkward designs.
When life looks so silly, it's hard not to cheer,
With every wild story, the world feels so near.

Light's Gentle Embrace

Sunlight dances on the floor,
Cats play tag, seeking more.
A shadow slips, a sudden sprawl,
Who knew a nap could take a fall?

Breezes tease the curtains wide,
The dog yawns, about to slide.
A squirrel peeks, then does a twirl,
Furry acrobat in a whirl!

Giggles burst from outside the gate,
Kids plotting mischief, oh, how great!
An ice cream cone, a sticky fight,
Sweet chaos in the summer light.

With every glance, a silly scene,
Home's a circus, yet serene.
Each moment's framed, a laughing face,
In light's embrace, a warm embrace.

Echoes of Laughter and Leaves

The wind whispers secrets in trees,
As squirrels chatter with carefree ease.
Laughter echoes from passersby,
Was that a giggle or a pie in the sky?

Bubbles float from a soapy bowl,
A toddler shouts, 'I'm on a roll!'
The dog spins round in pure delight,
Chasing shadows, a comical sight.

Children leap, laughter fills the air,
Each fall and tumble, a sassy flair.
The streetlamp flickers, a lamp in jest,
As shadows dance, they never rest.

In playful moments, we only see,
Echoes of joy that set us free.
Leaves crunch underfoot with pure delight,
As smiles abound, everything feels right.

Glances at the Untamed

The garden's wild, a riotous mood,
Weeds wear crowns, oh, how they brood!
A gnome tilts, looks slightly askew,
What secrets lie beneath the dew?

Watch the dog chase a flying leaf,
His leaps and bounds beyond belief.
With each twist, he claims his prize,
In this realm of doggy lies.

Birds squawk gossip from tangled vines,
Raccoons plotting, drawing up lines.
The mailman giggles, dodging a tie,
As chaos reigns, we all comply.

Framing life through a peek of shade,
Every glance reveals a masquerade.
In this world where wild things bloom,
Laughter stirs, dispelling gloom.

The Canvas of Ordinary Moments

A mug spills over, coffee's done,
Splatter art, oh, what fun!
The toast pops up, a glorious sight,
Jam-smeared smiles, morning light.

Chairs creak under tales retold,
The cat leaps high, feeling bold.
Sock puppets stage a grand debut,
Can a floor be a stage for two?

With crayons and laughter on the wall,
Creativity takes its colorful call.
Each scribble brings us a chuckle or two,
In a house where joy feels new.

Moments captured, so fleeting and bright,
An ordinary world, kissed with light.
Laughter paints each passing day,
On this canvas, come what may.

Living Color Outside the Borders

The neighbor's cat strikes a pose,
As if it knows, all eyes it grows.
Bouncing in the sun, proud and spry,
A furry king, no need to try.

The kids play tag, a joyous race,
While parents sip tea, with smiles on their face.
A dog joins in, barking for fun,
Chasing shadows, in the midday sun.

A flower pot tips, spills its cheer,
As petals dance, it draws us near.
The hummingbirds flit, all aglow,
In a chaotic ballet, stealing the show.

Laughter erupts from the crowded street,
As ice cream drips, oh what a treat!
Sidewalk chalk paints dreams and schemes,
Life's vivid canvas, bursting at the seams.

A Lens of Familiar Faces

The postman waves, he's got a grin,
Delivering smiles, it's always a win.
As he fumbles, a package takes flight,
Who knew that mail could be such a sight?

The old lady plants her garden with style,
Talks to her daisies, goes the extra mile.
While squirrels plot, in their tiny suits,
Planning a heist, of her prized fruits.

Children giggle, playing hopscotch lines,
Their laughter dances, like sunshine shines.
The rhythm of the day skips and twirls,
In this living film, a joyous swirl.

A jogger trips, then strikes a pose,
Rolling like a log, what a comedic close!
Every moment's gold, captured with grace,
Life's sitcom, in this lively space.

Everyday Epiphanies

The neighbor's dog chases a leaf,
Round and round, oh what a belief!
Who knew nature could spark such glee,
In a world so vast, it's silly, you see?

A toddler's tantrum, a grand affair,
Mom's patience tested, almost bare.
But then a bubble floats on by,
And suddenly all tears will dry.

A delivery guy slips, but recovers quick,
Turns the fall into a party trick.
With pizza in hand, he takes a bow,
Is this life? It sure shows how!

Sunset paints the sky with wild hues,
As neighbors wave, sharing the news.
In this mosaic of laughing faces,
Everyday magic, in humorous places.

The Heartbeat of the Outside

A raccoon rummages, what a sight!
Stealing scraps under the pale moonlight.
With little hands, it picks and pulls,
Life's cheeky thief, breaking the rules.

The neighbors grumble, with a grin,
As loud music spills from within.
Friday night plays a festive tune,
While the stars compete, for space and bloom.

Birds squawk loud, a silly retort,
As they flutter about, a bustling court.
Nature's gossip, woven with quirks,
In the laughter of life, nothing lurks.

And so we sit, with joy in our hearts,
Watching life unfold, a series of arts.
With quirks and giggles, we find our way,
In the warm embrace of a vibrant day.

Scenes Beyond the Safety Net

A dog in pajamas takes a leap,
While the cat in a hat watches, half-asleep.
Neighbors practice circus acts with flair,
As I sip my coffee and pretend not to stare.

A squirrel in a tutu daintily prances,
While toddlers attempt their big, bold dances.
A bird on a swing gives a squawk and a grin,
What wild antics the world shows, while I'm tucked in.

The mailman juggles letters with style,
While the kids play tag in a comical pile.
With every new scene, laughter erupts,
In this sitcom of life, joy is constructively cupped.

A grumpy old man shouts at the clouds,
While a tumble of laughter rolls from the crowds.
In every single moment, humor's the theme,
Outside my happy haven, life bursts at the seam.

Transients in the Frame

A giraffe drapes its neck on the fence,
While a neighbor complains, feeling tense.
A cactus is dressed in a colorful shawl,
As children tune up for a make-believe ball.

Delivery trucks dance to invisible beats,
As kids on their scooters rush down the streets.
An old lady dances, broom in hand,
With each twist and turn, she forms a new band.

A parade of bicycles zooms by with glee,
Waving at pigeons just trying to see.
In this spectacle, life seems to spin,
Each little moment a giggle within.

The UPS driver tips his hat with a wink,
As a toddler spills juice and turns bright pink.
With each clumsy mishap and joyous act,
The world's a silly stage, that's a fact!

Framed Moments of Light

A clock on the wall plays tricks with our minds,
As shadows dance lightly, the silliness binds.
A cat flips a switch, and the curtains collide,
Creating a scene none can easily hide.

Through the petals of daisies, a bee's in a race,
Chasing after the sunlight in this lively space.
Birds in their jackets are planning a flight,
While down below, bunnies avoid a good sight.

A postman takes selfies with inflatable toys,
While giggling kids unleash summer joys.
Each snapshot reveals a funny little tale,
Of the quirks and the laughs that never grow stale.

With props and strange costumes, the world comes alive,
In each silly moment, these smiles we derive.
Be it the whirligig wind or a jester's delight,
Life is framed in this fun, glorious light!

Secrets in the Glass

A raccoon in slippers seems quite out of place,
Peering through plants with a curious face.
A chubby old squirrel takes out its huge stash,
As I chuckle softly at nature's brash hash.

A child with a spoon juggles his lunch,
While a cat ponders whether to pounce or to munch.
Neighbors gossip loudly, soft laughter and sneers,
Each secret unveiled over snacks and cold beers.

A family of ducks waddles by in a line,
Each one wearing shades—oh, what a design!
As they strut with flair, it's a fashion parade,
And I can't help but grin at this scene they have made.

Through translucent boundaries, the madness unfolds,
With every glance given, a new story molds.
In this comical world where life's truly vast,
The funny little moments are forever amassed.

Melodies of the Universe

A cat on the sill, thinking it's grand,
While squirrels debate, forming a band.
The world's a stage, a comic display,
As birds tweet gossip about their day.

With toast in the air, a breakfast ballet,
And cereal spills, like confetti at play.
Mom's yelling 'Now!' at the dog in a race,
While kids dodge chaos with glee on their face.

The neighbor's lawn mower, a grumpy old tune,
Makes me laugh hard, under the bright afternoon.
Meanwhile, the fridge hums a jazzy refrain,
As I ponder a nap, but can't miss the game.

So blend these odd sounds, a raucous delight,
In this circus of life, everything feels right.
I raise my glass high, to the whimsy we find,
In this quirky abode, oh so well-defined.

Serenity Between the Bars

The dog in a dream, guarding his throne,
While the goldfish looks bored, sways all alone.
A tuneful old radio croons soft and low,
As I sip my tea, enjoying the show.

The couch tells tales of snacks gone awry,
While popcorn kernels jump, oh, what a sky!
TV's a circus, with laughter and shouts,
And I giggle along, without any doubts.

The lamp starts to flicker, a small disco light,
While the cat's practiced stealth, stalking at night.
Beneath the warm glow, the world feels just fine,
In this comical life, all the stars align.

So here in this space, absurdity reigns,
With moments that sparkle like shimmering planes.
A mirthful retreat from the stress of the day,
With smiles that remind me of joy in the fray.

Life Beyond the Threshold

The mailman arrives like a hero in disguise,
With junk mail and flyers, it's all quite the prize.
The porch light flickers, a ghost in the night,
While shadows perform in a silly moonlight.

Neighbors wave to each other with zest,
Exchanging their gossip, a hilarious fest.
Children chase fireflies, a dance of delight,
While laughter erupts in the warmth of twilight.

An old chair creaks, telling tales of its own,
While pots make a clang, like a rolling stone.
In the yard, a garden contest gets rough,
As weeds and the daffodils battle for fluff.

So here's to the joy, the madness outside,
Where life runs amok, and I can't help but bide.
With a wink and a nudge, let the wild times unfold,
In this land of bizarre, where life feels so bold.

A Glimmer of Normalcy

Morning sun stretches, tickling the floor,
While grandma's old cat guards the front door.
Pancakes flip high, like the kids in the air,
Laughing all harder than the sun's golden glare.

The dog's on a mission; he's found the lost sock,
And steers clear of trouble, like clock tock tock.
The kid on the swing yells, "I'm flying so high!"
While mom feigns a gasp, watching 'til he can fly.

The clock keeps on ticking, a reluctant timekeeper,
While the vacuum's a monster, creeping and deeper.
With crumbs on the floor, the kitchen's a mess,
But the joy in the chaos? Oh, what a success!

So let's raise a toast to this typical spree,
Of moments that dance and set laughter free.
In this perfect parade of the strange and the fun,
Where oddness is normal, life's never done.

Sights of Solitude

In a chair I sit with ease,
Watching squirrels chase the breeze.
One fell down and took a spin,
While birds just cackle—what a din!

The curtain flutters, blowing wide,
A curious cat attempts to hide.
With paws outstretched, she makes her claim,
On every shadow, every name.

Outside, a dog is on a quest,
To find the mailman, he's obsessed.
Delivery comes, the joy is clear,
He leaps and barks, with endless cheer.

A neighbor tumbles, trips, and rolls,
While another juggles popcorn bowls.
I snicker, sip my tea, what fun,
This play of life, oh, how it's spun.

Fragments of Sunlit Days

Sun spills gold across the floor,
A dance of dust, a slight roar.
The clock ticks slow, the world's a tease,
As time drips down like honey bees.

A little bird, so low and spry,
Decides to give the world a try.
He flaps the window, what a show,
Then lands right on my neighbor's toe.

A toddler's giggle breaks the air,
He tumbles over with no care.
His ice cream cone, a messy sight,
But oh, that joy, it's pure delight!

Outside, a dance of garden gnomes,
They wiggle weird in leafy homes.
As I observe their silly schemes,
I ponder life in vivid dreams.

The Unseen Symphony

The traffic hums a playful tune,
While I sit watching, afternoon.
A cat sings softly, 'Feed me now!'
While pigeons strut with grandiose vow.

A man in socks, mismatched and bright,
Does yoga moves—what a sight!
The grass beneath him sways and bends,
As onlookers chuckle, he transcends.

The ice cream truck plays its sweet song,
A kid runs fast, but it's all wrong.
He trips and lands with sticky hands,
While seagulls swoop with silly plans.

The laughter of life floats like a breeze,
As chairs creak softly, and branches tease.
Every moment's a giggling jest,
In this symphony of pure zest.

Hues of Dusk and Dawn

With dawn comes coffee and wide-open eyes,
The sky is painted in peachy sighs.
Bicycles whizz by with squeaky cheer,
As I savor laughter, brewed right here.

At dusk, the glow begins to play,
Neighbors out walking, enjoying the fray.
A dog with a sock escapes the leash,
While kids in capes declare, 'Release!'

The leaves dance lightly on gentle tunes,
While I sip tea and watch the cartoons.
A couple argues, then bursts into glee,
As their kid bounces around like a flea.

Stars pop out, like jokes in a night,
Each twinkle brings a delight so bright.
I'll sit here chuckling, the world unfolds,
In every scene, new laughter molds.

Secrets of the Pane

A squirrel with style, strikes a pose,
Dancing on branches, as the curtain close.
He steals my snack, with flair and glee,
I wonder if he's got a degree.

A bird chirps tales, in ruffled delight,
Spilling the tea on a cat's late-night.
I watch with a grin, they prance and sway,
While I sip my coffee, all in dismay.

Neighbors parade by in mismatched shoes,
Stumbling and laughing, with nothing to lose.
Their stories collide, like dreams of the night,
Who knew suburban life could be this bright?

The window frames laughter, a view so grand,
With sticky fingers and crumbs on the hand.
I vanish in giggles, lost in the spree,
Who knew my best friends were just outside me?

Beyond the Threshold of Comfort

A dog in a tutu, oh what a sight,
He chases his tail, with all of his might.
I grab for my phone, to snap and share,
But down he goes in a tumble, unaware.

The mailman arrives, brave as a knight,
Dressed in his armor, delivering might.
He dodges the barks, with a wink and a grin,
I cheer from my sofa, let the fun begin.

A child with a cape, flies past the door,
He claims he's a hero, needing much more.
With socks on his hands, he signals the fight,
Against an invisible foe, oh what a sight!

Behind the clear glass, a world full of cheer,
Where laughter and chaos collide, oh dear!
In the cozy nook, I sit with delight,
The outside antics make everything right.

A View Between Four Walls

A cat on the windowsill, batting a fly,
While pigeons plot mischief from up in the sky.
Both unaware of the audience here,
Who chuckle and snicker, as antics appear.

Kids jump on the trampoline, higher and higher,
Each bounce a new wish on a sprinkle of fire.
One lands like a rocket, all giggles and falls,
Their laughter escapes, bliss echoing the walls.

Gardening gloves toss dirt, like snow in mid-June,
An old man stands proud, a forgotten cartoon.
He talks to his flowers, they clearly can hear,
"Your blossoms are lovely!" I shout, full of cheer.

Here in my nook, with the heat of the sun,
I sip on some lemonade, life's funny rerun.
With quirks and odd wonders, I gaze and I grin,
These moments, my treasures, let the fun begin!

The Unseen Symphony

The wind whispers secrets, soft on my cheeks,
While neighbors debate what color's the peaks.
From glares to the giggles, a cacophony plays,
In this tiny theater, I'm lost in the craze.

A yapping pup claims the street as his own,
While a bird fluffs her feathers, feels right at home.
The rhythm of life beats both quick and slow,
In this charming oddity, the best show to know.

A bicycle zooms by, with a horn that won't quit,
"Watch out!" yells a friend, as he tumbles and flits.
The symphony swells, an orchestra found,
As laughter takes center, a sweet, joyful sound.

Behind this clear glass, the world takes its cue,
A unique performance, forever in view.
I chuckle and muse, at the scenes all around,
In this silent concert, funny tales abound.

Stories of the Unseen

A cat on a fence, so high and proud,
It watches the world, far from the crowd.
A dog spots the squirrel, it's quite the show,
With a leap and a bark, the chaos will grow.

The neighbor's hot dog, so charred and black,
An unsuspecting bird, comes in for a snack.
With a peck and a hop, it's a feast quite bizarre,
While the grill master sits, dreaming of gourmet stars.

Kids on bicycles, they zoom and slide,
With laughter that echoes, and no place to hide.
In the puddles they splash, like tiny bright frogs,
Unfazed by the clouds, they're just happy little dogs.

And there goes a lady, a hat full of flair,
She's got a pet turtle stuck in her hair.
With a wink and a giggle, she struts with pride,
In the grand play of life, she's the punchline, the guide.

A View from the Heart

An old man on a swing, just swaying so slow,
He tells tales to the breeze, only he seems to know.
His laughs echo softly, like a gentle breeze,
While his dog looks at him, like 'you're one of these.'

A couple walks by, all tangled in shoes,
They trip on the sidewalk, oh what a ruse.
With a giggle and shrug, they krinkle their nose,
Life's little stumbles, a dance, I suppose.

A child with a kite, it's stuck in a tree,
He yells to his dad, "Hey, come rescue me!"
With a ladder and laughter, they climb up so brave,
To free all the colors that the wind gave.

The postman rides by, with a grin on his face,
Delivering laughter, at a swift, breezy pace.
He waves to the neighbors, like a king on his throne,
In the theater of life, he's the jester, full-grown.

Tapestry of Everyday Life

The baker next door, with flour in hair,
Bakes bread like art, no detail is spare.
While customers cheer, for the loaves piled tall,
They leave with a smile, the best treat of all.

A toddler with crayons, colors the sky,
Drawing purple sunsets, oh my, oh my!
And the mom shakes her head, with a giggle so bright,
"Just wait till it washes, it'll give me a fright!"

A lawnmower sputters, then stops with a cough,
And the neighbor yells out, "Time to trim, not scoff!"
With a laugh and a wave, they bond in the weeds,
In this tapestry woven, where humor proceeds.

The mail brings a letter, with stickers galore,
From a cousin who swears, it's all tales of lore.
"Uncle Joe caught a fish, it was this big, I swear!"
But the real fun is waiting, for April's wild air.

The Colors of Familiar Strangers

A bird on a branch, with an attitude bold,
Sings all the wrong notes, like a tale old.
With a flourish it hops, as if in a play,
While the trees just sway gently, in their leafy ballet.

The jogger trips twice, in bright neon shoes,
He laughs with the bushes, ignoring their blues.
Each tumble a dance, each sweat a delight,
He waves to the flowers, "You're my spirit tonight!"

An elderly lady, with a purse like a ship,
Swats her poodle's nose, gives his cheek a quick flip.
While he looks quite offended, she just starts to grin,
It's a daily routine, the kind you can't win.

A squirrel steals an acorn, with flair and with speed,
Darts across lawns, it's the wildest of deeds.
While the onlookers chuckle at his crafty, sly game,
In the colors of strangers, we all share the same fame.

Scents of the Changing Seasons

The aroma of pies wafts in the air,
Leaves turning golden, a colorful affair.
Socks in the dryer, a strange kind of dance,
Even the cat thinks it's time for a prance.

Pumpkin spice lattes, they flood the street,
While kids hunt for candy with eyes so sweet.
Jumping in puddles, splashes like cheers,
Winter's cold whispers, bringing out fears.

Roses are smelling like chocolate today,
Or is that just lunch? I can't really say.
As seasons keep shifting, it all seems a joke,
No bedazzled fruits, just a veggie cloak.

Mismatched socks and days run amok,
Swatting at flies with the might of a rock.
This strange little cycle, it never grows old,
Seasons live on with stories retold.

The Magic of Everyday Moments

Waking to sunshine, the toast pops up,
A cereal circus in a plastic cup.
Dancing with dishes, while dodging some grime,
Finding lost socks, what a terrible crime!

Conversations with mugs, they spill all the tea,
And plants seem to gossip, who knew they could be?
Life's little wonders, like crumbs on the floor,
Even the toaster is ready to score.

Falling asleep with a book on my face,
The cat looks on, judging my grace.
Miracles hidden in crumbs and in dust,
Everyday magic, it's truly a must.

Moments like these, they tickle my heart,
Crafting grand tales from the smallest part.
Sipping on life, there's humor in strife,
Finding the laughter makes joy come to life.

The World's Canvas Painted in Light

Splashes of colors from curtains so bright,
A rainbow of chaos fills up my sight.
The clock ticks' giggles in a silent ballet,
While dust motes waltz like they're on holiday.

The sun paints the walls in hues of pure cheer,
As shadows play tag with each passing year.
Framed memories chuckle, they wink from their perch,
Like mischief-makers in a sunlit church.

Then comes the dusk with a wink and a nudge,
And whispers of dreams, a cozy warm grudge.
Life is a canvas where laughter is strewn,
Each brush of a moment, a bright afternoon.

Stars dazzle softly in a twinkling parade,
Light dances through windows, a whimsical charade.
With every glance, there's a story to share,
In this quirky gallery, life's wonder does flare.

As the Day Unfolds

Morning light peeks, a mischievous greet,
As socks find their mates in a wild little feat.
Coffee spills over, and so does my plan,
This day has been waiting, but where do I stand?

Chasing my shadow, it giggles and runs,
Pretending to work while I'm searching for puns.
The clock strikes humor, it's a comical race,
Will I ever triumph in this silly space?

A cat on my lap and a dog at my feet,
This crew of companions, it's impossible to beat.
As moments unravel like a wild tumble,
Laughter echoes loud, in chaos I stumble.

The day keeps on turning, with giggles and glee,
As I juggle my tasks—tea, laundry, and me.
In the silly parade of my normal, routine,
Every little moment becomes a grand scene.

www.ingramcontent.com/pod-product-compliance
Lightning Source LLC
Chambersburg PA
CBHW060123230426
43661CB00003B/311